I0415505

Icicle

First published 2012 by Rough Little Books
www.roughlittlebooks.co.uk

Copyright © 2012 Christopher Bourne

The right of Christopher Bourne to be identified as the author of this work has been
asserted by him in accordance with the Copyright and Patents Act 1988.

All rights reserved. No part of this publication may be reproduced, transmitted or stored
in a retrieval system, in any form or by any means, without permission in writing from
Rough Little Books.

ISBN: 978-1-291-09477-0

Icicle

Christopher Bourne

Danish Text by Henrik Magnild Husum

Act 1: Look-out Station Arctic Circle 500km north of Tasiilaq

Act 2: Look-out Station Arctic Circle 500km north of Tasiilaq

One week later.

Act 3: Look-out Station Arctic Circle 500km north of Tasiilaq

Three weeks later.

Act 4: Look-out Station Arctic Circle 500km north of Tasiilaq

Three weeks later.

Time: present

Cast

Paul Cartwright

Late forties, tough lean and not happy being alone for so long.
   English

Martin Illemann

Danish, late forties, remote and cut off from the world. He is
   obsessed with work, it's his whole life.

On the video screen

Beth Cartwright (Paul's wife)

Elliot Cartwright (his seventeen year old son)

Jesper (Danish logistics' commander & friend of Martin's)

Sharon (Elizabeth's mother)

Ida Illemann (Paul's mother)

Socrates (Paul's Greek boyfriend)

Mr King (Paul's boss)

John (Facility logistics)

Copyright © 2012 Rough Little Books

Act 1
Scene 1

The sound of the whistling Arctic wind whipping outside. Lights up on a stage divided into two; there is a door, stage right, close to the door, there is a single bed, neatly made, at the foot of the bed sits a small white box which, we discover later, contains stuff belonging to Paul Cartwright. On the opposite side of the stage is a desk, upon which sits a lap top and a phone earpiece; two chairs are next to this desk. Above the desk is a huge screen. As the lights get brighter there is a beeping sound and the laptop and the enormous screen comes to life. The audience see the screen come to life and a woman, Elizabeth is looking into the camera, into the room. She is agitated and moving about. We can see she is in a nice flat somewhere.

ELIZABETH: Paul, Paul are you there? *(She talks to someone she is with, she is sitting in her warm flat in London, communicating by web cam with her husband, who is stationed in the Arctic Circle.)* Christ, what time is it? Yes, I know, I told him Tuesday I'd be calling. Just keep quiet for a moment. *(She turns to the camera and looks, she can see into the room of the set. Then she looks to her left and speaks)* I've no idea where he is, he could be out on the ice. No, he does that in the mornings, what time is it? I know it's two hours behind. But what time is it here now any way? Well, he should be there, I haven't got all morning; I've got the shopping to do.

The door stage right bursts open and the wind howls louder and white flakes of snow billow in. Paul enters wrapped up against the Arctic cold. He has goggles, a hat and gloves on, his mouth is covered. He walks past the laptop and screen.

ELIZABETH: *(To Paul)* There you are! I told you Tuesday I'd be calling now.

Paul walks to the bed, and starts to remove all his layers. In quick succession he strips down to his underwear, revealing a thin, lean body. He puts his coat, hat, gloves and other thermals down, as Elizabeth talks on. His is wearing his underpants and he adjusts it as he continues to listen to Elizabeth.

ELIZABETH: We've got a problem, your son wants to go to a party with his friends and I've told him he can't. Not that you'd be interested, seeing as I have to remind you of his existence every time we speak.

ELLIOT: HELLO! DAD! I love you.

ELIZABETH: Stop shouting in my ear, young man. Your Father won't let you go and that's that.

All this time Paul has been making faces and busying himself trying to buy time, on the other side of the room, hoping he'll avoid the ensuing confrontation. Finally he moves in front of the screen; his son and wife are still fighting. For a moment he stares at them and then coughs. He pulls on his underpants, it's all he's wearing now. Elizabeth is stern, as Elliot looks over her shoulder, smiling.

ELIZABETH: For god's sake Paul, put some clothes on.

He reaches over and pulls his sweater around his shoulders. Mother and son carry on arguing. Paul rolls his eyes and takes out a flask and, secretly, knocks back a swing of Brandy, one of his favourites.

ELIZABETH: I hope that's not alcoholic.

Paul's eyes pop open and he shakes his head.

ELIZABETH: You know what the doctor's report said last year, you've got to cut back on the booze, remember?

ELLIOT: Oh, Dad, please let me go to the party.

ELIZABETH: You're not nineteen yet and until you are you'll do as I, we say.

ELLIOT: It's the end of year party for school Dad, and my year's been invited to go as well, isn't that cool?

Paul nods his head and smiles.

ELIZABETH: He wants to go with this boy he's become friends with, he's called Andrew. He's two year's older and you know what boys of that age can get up to.

Paul rolls his eyes.

ELIZABETH: It's all very well for you sitting up there, in Greenland, all on your own, leaving me to run the household, raising him all on my own. You said you'd only do this job for a couple of years and here we are, fifteen bloody years later...

ELLIOT: We see him for holidays... don't we? Dad?

Paul nods and smiles at the screen again, taking another swig.

ELIZABETH: I don't want him to go to this party and that's that and I want you to tell him. You got that? What are you drinking?

Paul takes another swig and puts the flask down, wiping his beard.

PAUL: (*To Elizabeth*) Have you met this Andrew?

ELIZABETH: Yes, of course I have, he's been here to dinner a number of times. What's in the flask?

PAUL: Do you like him?

ELIZABETH: Yes, I do. But that's not the point…

PAUL: Elliot, your Dad says you can go to the party.

ELIZABETH: What?

ELLIOT: Wow! Thanks Dad, I love you. Yippee!

PAUL: You too… (Smiling broadly)

ELIZABETH: You can't do this…Paul…

PAUL: Sorry Elizabeth, I've got another call coming through I'll call you later.

He reaches over to the computer, while Elizabeth rants on.

ELIZABETH: This is outrageous, you don't help one bit, where were you when the roof leaked, when Elliot needed braces, got beat up, went to sixth form, where? you've done nothing for this family. Nothing…

PAUL: Except pay for everything you've just mentioned and more.

ELIZABETH: Don't you dare cut me…

He switches the computer off, and moves to the other side of the room with the flask and he lies down on the bed. For a moment he lies there listening to the wind howling outside. We notice that he twitches and fidgets a lot, and he mutters under his breath.

PAUL: et dum seminat quaedam ceciderunt secus viam et venerunt volucres et comederunt ea

And whilst he soweth some fell by the way side, and the birds of the air came and ate them up.

He sits up on the bed, looks about, lies back down again, and then repeats this movement. He sits up rubbing himself, as though he were cold. He goes over to a control console on the far wall stage left. He looks at it and then bashes it with his fist. He goes to the desk and taps at the laptop.

PAUL: Snow base Alpha Tango, calling Control. Do you read? Snow base Alpha Tango, calling Control. Do you read?

He waits for a moment and the light from the computer screen flashes to life. It's John; the man in London.

JOHN: Very funny Paul, you know those commands went out with the last century.

PAUL: Some of the old fashioned ways help me stay grounded. Hate to cut to the point but, as you can imagine, I've quite a few points in my life as it is, what with the point of sitting here every day watching an empty sky for the last fifteen years.

JOHN: Thank god for that.

PAUL: And the jagged point of the freezing cold and the tiny points of snow pricking all over my face when I have to go out and bang together the lousy equipment you lot send me to patch onto the obsolete crap you bought five years ago from an aging American company, to keep the oil pumping...

JOHN: What is it Paul?

PAUL: The reactor looks like it's on it's last legs and apart from the fact, that, as you know, I won't be sad to see the end of another nuclear power station in the world, I do need this particular reactor as this one is directly related to my survival so, if you don't want to feel the prick of my knife in your back when I track you down in sunny London, you'd better send me the parts I ordered three weeks ago now, so I don't freeze to death.

JOHN: I'm just checking that order…

PAUL: Good.

JOHN: According to my records they were despatched two weeks ago and you should have had them by now.

PAUL: I don't think I'd be calling you now if I had, do you?

JOHN: Err…

PAUL: DO YOU?

JOHN: Christ, Paul, it's not my fault the order's not gone through. I sent it out, I promise. I'm checking the order on my invoice now. Yes, I did, it went, so the problem is down at the warehouse, so there's no need to shout.

Paul walks to centre stage front and looks at the audience. His twitching calms down slightly, but we're not sure if he's going to pounce on us or not. He holds a copy of the bible in his hand, having picked it up from his cupboard on the way down front.

PAUL: I think you'd be shouting too if all there was between you and the freezing cold of the Arctic Circle was a little pen-pushing shit like you sitting on his fat, warm arse in Central London.

JOHN: I'll sort it…

Turning to look at John, he goes back to the laptop.

PAUL: Today! I'll call you later this afternoon.

Paul pushes the button and the computer screen goes blank.

PAUL: Arsehole.

He goes over to the bed and strips off some more down to just his underpants. He plays with his bollocks. He pushes a few buttons on his laptop and settles down to staring at the screen. He does this for a moment or two and then gets up and does some press ups.

PAUL: Ten, eleven, twelve, thirteen, fourteen, fifteen. Come on
    you lazy swine, more. (*He does some more*).

He then steps to the front of the stage, and squints. The wind howls louder. Effectively, he's looking out the window onto the arctic.

PAUL:

Great white beauty,
great white hell,
I stand here before you
watching you swell.
Once I held my head aloft
Above the hum and throng.
Turned my face towards the north
Chiselling my brave song.

The video buzzer rings again and John's face appears on the screen.

JOHN: I've verified the order and it will, definitely be with you
    the day after tomorrow.

PAUL: Are you sure about this, John?

JOHN: Well, er yes, I am. Didn't you get the email that was sent to you last Tuesday?

PAUL: Email? What email? I get loads of them all of the bloody time, so you'll have to be a little more specific.

JOHN: It was dated the 29th November.

PAUL: Wait.

He goes to the laptop turning it around so he can access the email.

PAUL: I have forty-six emails that day. What am I looking for? I responded to all of them by the way.

JOHN: Er, one that's headed, 'Change of use.'

Paul looks through them.

PAUL: No, nothing like that, send it again, now.

JOHN: Sure, right away.

Paul sits back and waits.

JOHN: It's gone.

Paul picks at his balls.

JOHN: Do you have to do that in front of me?

PAUL: What?

JOHN: That.

PAUL: When you come in from -45C to 25C it can feel a little too hot. Makes everything prickly and itchy.

He stops and takes a swig from the bottle.

JOHN: Hope that's fruit juice. You know the regulations.

PAUL: It's here. (*He reads and is shocked by something*) This can't be right. Says this place is being shut down.

JOHN: Well, it doesn't say that for sure. They're thinking about changing the use of the place.

PAUL: Why wasn't I told sooner?

JOHN: I told you I sent the email last Tuesday.

PAUL: And I've just told you I never got the damn thing. You've always had a hearing problem. What are you playing at?

JOHN: There's no need to get personal.

PAUL: You lying little shit.

JOHN: Don't swear at me. I won't tolerate you swearing at me.

PAUL: You never sent that email. Did you?

JOHN: There's something else you should know.

PAUL: You're replacing me here?

JOHN: No, there's someone on their way to you to oversee the change over or… closure.

PAUL: What? Who? Who's on their way here? I don't want anyone here.

JOHN: Just follow orders.

PAUL: I don't want anyone else here.

JOHN: Speak to Mr King.

PAUL: (*Panicked*) Send them back.

JOHN: I can't.

PAUL: (*A little hysterical*) Send them back.

JOHN: Calm down.

PAUL: (*Shouting*) Send them back!

JOHN: I'll hang up if you do that again.

PAUL: I don't need any one in my hair, especially when it comes to clearing up out of here, I can do that on my own.

JOHN: I'm just following orders.

PAUL: You can tell who ever it is to turn around and piss off back to where they came from. I can't believe you'd do this to me, after all the years we've worked together.

JOHN: Why can't you? Just look at you ranting like a mad man. I can't deal with your temper and shouting. I never have. I thought you religious ones were supposed to be all peace and harmony.

PAUL: Don't question my beliefs.

JOHN: And I knew this would upset you.

PAUL: Too right Judas...

Paul slams down on the laptop, severing the signal. He picks up the laptop and shouts abuse at it, swinging it around the room.

PAUL: Fucking little bastard shits. Piss ants, pricks, morons, and twats.

The video phone rings and rings and flicks to life in the middle of his rant.

PAUL: You expect me to jump now you tight arsed fucked up, twat pissers…

KING: Mr Cartwright, calm down.

PAUL: Don't you Mr me, you conceited bastard.

KING: Mr King to you. Paul, if you don't calm down I'll have you forcibly removed when the overseer arrives on Thursday. And that wouldn't be a good way to end, now would it?

PAUL: Are you threatening me, Mr King? Is that the reason for this 'courtesy call, Mr King? Nervous, I know too much, is that it, Mr King?

KING: I've been instructed to talk you through the changes that have been made.

PAUL: Why wasn't I consulted? I've been sitting up here all these years; didn't any of you hotheads think that I might be useful in helping to decide what to do with it?

KING: You know the decisions for this sort thing come from higher up.

PAUL: Don't military me, Mr King. Big Business has no jurisdiction here and you know it. The Danish Government has the last say.

KING: It's the Danes who've made this decision. Not us. They're saying that there's no justification for the expense of a facility such as the one you're in. They want to investigate the possibility of changing the work you do up there. So, they're sending one of their top specialists to help you assess the job in hand and report back to them at the end of the month.

PAUL: What about all the equipment?

KING: Quite possibly it will be used for the new job.

PAUL: What is this new job?

KING: Climate monitoring. Oil research.

PAUL: You mean searching for oil. Oh, Christ, everything would have to be re-calibrated. The whole lot, all of it re-done, re-worked, fine tuned. It's a lot of work.

KING: Don't give me a hard time Paul, after all I've done for you over the years, it's thanks to me that you've got to stay up there on your own as it is, you know the regulations.

PAUL: Yes, yes, I know the regulations 'no personnel are allowed to do a solitary position for any more than four consecutive months.' But it sounds like I won't be working for you any more.

KING: I still work for the company, the Danes pay more. And I still pay your bills. We all think you're not right in the head anyway being able to stay in that place from one year to the next. It's only because you've always been so efficient, that I stick my neck out like this.

PAUL: (*Pulling a face*) Nothing wrong with me, sir.

KING: You can do the job.

PAUL: Then my arse is carted out of here and that's the end of my job.

KING: I'm not saying that, you're very good at your job.

PAUL: I work alone.

KING: We appreciate your good work, Paul, that's why you're allowed to get away with murder.

PAUL: Thought that was because I work with you.

KING: You'll be expected to present a preliminary report on any observations you might have made or will make between now and Thursday, on any weather variations, if any.

PAUL: What are you on about? I started submitting those reports a year ago. Read them. It's all in there. The ice is melting, there's no permafrost this year and the polar bears are becoming a problem as there's nothing for them to eat except me.

KING: I want a new report ready by Thursday morning.

The screen goes blank.

PAUL: And fuck you too. Fucking piss head, fuck wit, tossed brained, bug fucked, moron mouthed prick.

He swigs from his bottle and opens his bible muttering to himself.

BLACKOUT

Act 1
Scene 2

From blackout the sounds of bins and rubbish being ransacked can be heard. Then there is a terrible growl of a large animal. Loud banging is heard and a small light is flicked on. Paul is lying in bed, rubbing his eyes; the noises have woken him up. The growls and noises get louder and more menacing. He sits up in bed as the door behind him is bashed and thumped, he swings round his haunches. The growling is just outside the door. He sits in the gloom, waiting, listening, and hoping the polar bear doesn't come in the room. He reaches under his pillow looking for something, the wind howls and the door bangs about, but no animal appears. He gets up and goes to the box at the end of the bed and rummages around. He pulls out a huge hunting knife that glitters in the light, he keeps hold of this then reaches in the box again and pulls out a revolver. He throws the knife back in the box.

PAUL: (*Muttering under his breath*) interim fames omnem terram vehementer premebat

In the mean time the famine was heavy upon all the land.

Slowly, he gets to his feet and moves towards the door to make sure it's secure, there is another growl and he stands still, breathing heavily, terrified. Even with the gun he'd be no match for a full grown polar bear.

PAUL: Go to sleep, Jacob, my friend. Sleep, sleep.

The scratchings and rumblings die down again and he dives for the door, pulling it shut. The polar bear roars outside, Paul, rocks himself on the floor as the scratching and banging disappear.

PAUL: (*Muttering under his breath*) interim fames omnem terram vehementer premebat

In the mean time the famine was heavy upon all the land.

BLACKOUT

ACT 1
Scene 3

Lights up as Paul prepares for the day, the radio is playing some mindless tune, and he hums along to it. He turns on his laptop and writes in his report book.

PAUL: mense secundo septima et vicesima die mensis arefacta est terra

In the second month, the seven and twentieth day of the month, the earth was dried.

Paul's trembling is quite marked; he almost makes the room shake. He drops his pen.

PAUL: Fucking, piss head, fuck wit, toss brained, bug fuck, moron mouthed prick.

Suddenly, the web cam rings and Paul taps a button and the screen comes to life, it is his son, Elliot. He looks rough, dishevelled, he's very uptight and he sniffs a lot.

ELLIOT: Hi, Dad.

PAUL: Elliot, you look terrible.

ELLIOT: I've just finished my mock exams.

PAUL: How'd it go?

ELLIOT: I know the work but when it comes to taking exams I get all nervous and I make a mess of it.

PAUL: You'll be all right, son, don't worry. How's your mother?

ELLIOT: We're all fine. How's work?

PAUL: The same, well, no, I can't tell you remember?
(*Joking*)I've signed the Official Secrets Act and I'll have to...

ELLIOT: (*Wan smile*) shoot me, yes, I know.

PAUL: I've got a new job, possibly.

ELLIOT: (*Pleased*) You're leaving Greenland?

PAUL: (*Whispers*) Well, no, I'm not sure, I know you'd be happy
for me to leave here, but it pays well and your Mother would
find it hard to adjust to a pauper's wage.

ELLIOT: She's out with Graham, at the moment.

PAUL: She still seeing him?

ELLIOT: Yeah, she says they're just friends now, he's a right
wanker.

PAUL: (*Playing*) That's no way to talk about your Mum's
boyfriend, I mean ex-boyfriend.

ELLIOT: You're lucky, you never met him.

PAUL: Now I never will.

ELLIOT: There's someone new on the scene, I think, I know
when Mum's 'dating' someone, she gets all different, and
'chummy.' (*There is a long pause, as they sit looking at each
other. Paul tries to control his agitation and unease by
holding his left hand still with his right. Elliot fails to notices
this, as he's trying to hold it together his end, he's a coke
head.*) I'd like you to leave that place. It's not good for you to
be all alone like that and I miss you, Dad.

PAUL: Sorry about your birthday party, I couldn't get the leave.

ELLIOT: (*Sadly*) Yeah, I know, I understand.

PAUL: What are you doing at the weekend?

ELLIOT: Going for my driving lesson.

PAUL: Don't worry about it, you'll pass this time.

ELLIOT: And if I do, can I have that car you promised?

PAUL: I said I'd buy you a car but not the one you want, it's too expensive. I thought more along the lines of an old banger.

ELLIOT: Aw, that's terrible; all my friends have brand new cars. Nathaniel has a brand new Ford.

PAUL: His Dad's a barrister.

ELLIOT: Does it have to be so old?

PAUL: 1999's not so long ago.

ELLIOT: It's so last Century.

PAUL: Who's going to help you choose it?

ELLIOT: Graham's offered.

PAUL: He has, has he? Well that's nice…

ELLIOT: He has no taste, look at this picture of him.

He holds a picture to the camera and we see a man in a really bad suit, grinning inanely at us. Paul and Elliot laugh.

ELLIOT: Look at him.

PAUL: Do you get on with him?

ELLIOT: I just ignore him.

PAUL: You're good at that.

ELLIOT: Dad!

PAUL: Remember that time I told you not to go down the side street on your bike?

ELLIOT: I still have the scar.

PAUL: You didn't listen to me then.

ELLIOT: You were so shocked.

PAUL: You should have held still when they were stitching your arm.

ELLIOT: That big fat nurse sat on my head to hold me down.

PAUL: Your screaming scared me to death.

ELLIOT: That was a good holiday. (*Pause*) Is that why you stopped coming home?

There is a change in the atmosphere as Paul looks at his son.

PAUL: No, it was nothing to do with you.

ELLIOT: Not even making you stay. I couldn't even do that either, could I?

There is a long pause.

PAUL: I'll be home next month and I promise, I'll sit you down and explain everything to you. You're old enough to hear it now and, hopefully, understand.

ELLIOT: Tell me now.

PAUL: No, I want to sit down, buy you a drink; and not talk through this damn machine. It's horrible communicating like this.

ELLIOT: It's been the only way I've spoken to you in over a year.

PAUL: What I have to say must be done face to face. Are you all right?

ELLIOT: Yes, I'm great. There's nothing to worry about I promise. Mum will he home soon, shall I tell her to call you?

PAUL: Yes. And tell your Mum to take you round and send me the bill for the car, when you've passed your test.

ELLIOT: Thanks, Dad. I've got to go and put the tree up.

PAUL: That's nice.

ELLIOT: You know Mum, she likes it.

PAUL: Are you going anywhere for New Year's?

ELLIOT: A bunch of us are going to a club in town.

PAUL: You'd better not be driving Elliot.

ELLIOT: No, I'm not, Nathaniel is.

PAUL: All right, I'll speak to you later.

ELLIOT: Bye Dad.

The screen goes blank and, for a moment, Paul sits there swallowing something hard. Collapsing on the table, trembling, he fights back a sob and a sigh.

He misses his son and hates being away from him. He picks up his bible and flicks through it, closing it and then...

PAUL: congregatique sunt per singulas civitates oppida et loca ut extenderent manum contra inimicos et persecutores

And they gathered themselves together in every city, and town, and place, to lay their hands on their enemies, and their persecutors.

He pushes a button and the screen comes to life. It is the outside of the building he is sitting in. We see the snow and cold, then the image flips and we see the other way and in the distance a lone polar bear trods back and forth, keeping a bleary eye on the look out station.

PAUL: Jacob, my friend, are you back again? You old bugger. We've run out of meat. I'll get some more for you.

The polar bear rises up on his hind legs, as if he had heard what Paul had said. The video phone buzzes and Mr King is again on line.

KING: Morning Paul, how are you?

PAUL: Fine.

KING: I'm confirming that the Danish scientist is on his way to see you now and should be with you in the next twenty-four hours. We expect you to co-operate totally with him.

PAUL: I will, I may not agree with everything you do but I at least get on with it. Would you make sure that my order of pork is included in this shipment.

KING: You eat a lot of pork up there.

PAUL: So, who's this imminent Danish scientist you're sending me?

KING: He's just been removed from Athens where he's in charge of the Danish Mediterranean Disease Centre in Greece.

PAUL: Why was he chosen for his job, if all he knows about are bugs? They could have sent Kristian instead, he's good.

KING: Martin has a lot of experience developing facilities. He created some of the new equipment that's to be installed into your station.

PAUL: Martin who?

KING: Illemann, Doctor Martin Illemann.

Paul looks slightly pained and drained. His twitching almost makes his hair fall out. His eyes are wild with panic and terror.

PAUL: How old is he?

KING: *(Looking through the file on Paul)* Forty-eight trained at…

PAUL: Warwick University and the Danish Marine Institute 1983 to 1986.

KING: You know him?

PAUL: Yes, yes I do…

He has the wide-eyed look of a caged animal.

BLACKOUT

END OF ACT 1

Act 2
Scene 1

Lights up on stage. The TV screen is showing white noise and sitting in front of it is Martin Illemann, a tall, lean Dane. Intense and rather handsome. He's trying to get the videophone to work and he speaks in Danish and curses.

MARTIN: Satans til åndsvage tingest.

Fuck, this stupid thing.

He pushes another button and a disembodied voice is heard, in Danish. It is Jesper.

JESPER: Kom nu Martin, det er jo bare en enkelt dippedut.

Come on Martin, it's just one knob. (*He laughs*)

MARTIN: Shut up Jesper. This place is so untidy.

The screen crackles and fizzes.

JESPER: Nearly there.

The screen flashes to life and we see Jesper, blonde and Nordic.

MARTIN: Look at it all.

JESPER: Where's Paul?

MARTIN: He's collecting core samples from the glacier.

JESPER: How's it been?

MARTIN: He's said three words to me since I arrived here three days ago.

JESPER: What were they?

MARTIN: Hello, move and goodnight.

Jesper laughs.

JESPER: I expect it was a shock for him too. Is he cute?

MARTIN: Sadly he is; I hoped he'd be a great, big, fat bastard by now.

JESPER: It's going to be hard for you to keep your hands off him then?

MARTIN: Funny! Not if his personalities as evil as it has been.

JESPER: Did he pull a face when you fucked him?

MARTIN: Only when I did it from behind.

Jesper laughs, as Paul enters.

JESPER: You won't be able to keep your hands off him.

Du vil ikke kunne holde dine fingre fra ham.

The screen goes blank. Martin carries on working and Paul ignores him. Another message comes through as Paul walks off; it is Socrates, Martin's 22 year old beautiful, Greek boyfriend.

SOCRATES: Hi.

Martin looks round to see if Paul is still in the room.

MARTIN: I've told you not to call during the day.

SOCRATES: I wanted to make sure that I had the correct number for the ATM machine from your bank?

MARTIN: I wrote it on the paper I gave you.

SOCRATES: I lost it.

Paul peeks in trying to not be seen but we see he is listening.

MARTIN: Good god, where?

SOCRATES: I don't know, somewhere in the house. When are you coming home?

MARTIN: I've told you, I'm here for as long as it takes. There's nothing I can do about it.

SOCRATES: But this is stupid, what am I going to do?

MARTIN: What you usually do.

SOCRATES: I'm not talking about that again; I told you what I think.

MARTIN: Yes, and what part of 'I don't agree,' don't you understand?

They sit there in silence. The image flickers and flashes, it is a bad connection in more ways than one.

SOCRATES: It's just sex, Martin.

MARTIN: I can't separate it. And I don't want anyone in my flat while I am away and certainly not in my bed.

SOCRATES: You talk like a girl.

MARTIN: My feelings are my feelings and you should respect them, Socrates. When are you going to get it right?

SOCRATES: Right? You talk to me like I'm a child.

MARTIN: You said I 'talk like a girl,' that's not respecting my feelings, is it?

SOCRATES: I was only joking, lighten up.

MARTIN: You weren't joking.

SOCRATES: I was.

MARTIN: How are your Danish lessons coming?

SOCRATES: Terrible. Come home.

MARTIN: We'll talk about this later, I've got work to do.

SOCRATES: Always work…

MARTIN: Remember that the next time you go shopping.

The screen goes blank. Paul has heard most of it; he walks in clearing his throat making sure that Martin knows he is there. Paul busies himself at the laptop, checking the outside. He is withdrawn. The two men ignore each other, going about their various tasks. But every now and then Martin steals a look at Paul.

PAUL: How old is he?

MARTIN: Who?

PAUL: The boyfriend.

Martin looks at him, weighing up what he's going to say.

MARTIN: Twenty-three.

Paul laughs aloud.

PAUL: You deserve everything you get.

MARTIN: Explain…

PAUL: You're old enough to be his Dad. You've practically got to potty train him.

MARTIN: That's part of the attraction.

PAUL: Potty training? A lot of hard work if you ask me.

MARTIN: His incompleteness? I get to shape him, mold him.

PAUL: (*Angry*) Who do you think you are; God? I've got a son and I don't feel that way.

MARTIN: Maybe you should, you have a son?

PAUL: He's seventeen. He's not available.

Martin shoots him a look. The remark was mean and uncalled for.

MARTIN: Let's limit the talk to work, shall we? This data's been checked, verified? I assume.

PAUL: Yes, by me.

MARTIN: No one else checks it?

PAUL: No, never. They trust me.

MARTIN: So, no one checks your mistakes?

PAUL: There aren't any.

MARTIN: How do you know? This needs to be checked and then double checked. It helps to weed out mistakes, anomalies.

PAUL: I don't make them.

MARTIN: That's ridiculous. I want all the data from the last month and we're both going to sit down and double check it.

PAUL: You do it.

MARTIN: We're both going to do it.

PAUL: You can't pull rank on me.

MARTIN: As the representative of the Company I out rank you and you must do what order.

PAUL: 'You must do what I order.' You tried that with me over twenty years ago, it didn't work then and it certainly won't work now.

He storms off.

MARTIN: (*Shouting after him*) The data...

Paul re-appears carrying eight CDs; he dumps them on the desk.

PAUL: The last month you said.

MARTIN: Where are you going?

PAUL: To take the measurements for today.

Paul walks back out again. Martin sits for a moment. He stares at the computer screen. We hear the door slam as Paul goes out into the cold. Then we hear a growl and a roar, a door slams and Paul comes running back in.

PAUL: Jacob's out there again.

MARTIN: Who?

PAUL: Jacob, the polar bear.

MARTIN: What do you expect? We're in the Arctic Circle.

PAUL: He's getting bolder.

MARTIN: Desperate, he's probably starving.

PAUL: He's not eating me.

MARTIN: (*Smiling*) Probably not! Not enough fat.

Paul has been rummaging in the desk and he produces a revolver.

MARTIN: Don't shoot it.

PAUL: I'm not; I just fire over his head to scare him off.

MARTIN: Does it work?

PAUL: Well, yes, nearly always. He wants his meat. I've been feeding him pork for the last year or two.

MARTIN: Christ, it's not a pet.

PAUL: He can be very gentle with me.

MARTIN: Are you mad? It's a wild animal.

PAUL: He's my friend.

MARTIN: Don't get too close to it.

PAUL: I don't, I chuck the pork at him.

MARTIN: You should get danger money.

PAUL: Make the recommendation, you're in charge.

Martin ignores him and turns on the viewer screen, the snowy exterior is seen.

MARTIN: He seems to have gone.

PAUL: He's round back, the camera stopped working since he took a swipe at it last month.

Paul moves to go outside as Martin turns the image off.

PAUL: Squeamish?

MARTIN: Saving power.

Paul is out the door Martin sits there, the wind howling. There's a roar and two gunshots are heard, one after another. Martin stands up and listens, waiting, trembling. There is silence and silence. The radio crackles to life.

PAUL: (*VO*) It's all right; I chased him off.

Martin is visibly relieved but doesn't know why. He goes back to the desk and picks up the CDs. He opens the first one and puts it into the computer. He looks at the screen, then back at the door, works, back at the door, to the screen. He picks up the radio.

MARTIN: Paul! Come in Paul...

He goes to the front of the stage and looks out the window. He mutters something under his breath. We hear...

MARTIN: Paul...

BLACKOUT

Act 2
Scene 2

Lights up to find Paul and Martin sitting around drinking, not a good idea but all their work for the day has been finished. From the way they're sitting you can tell they're quite drunk, and there's a sexual energy throbbing in the air, helped by the fact that they're both sitting around in only long johns.

MARTIN: I got out as soon as I could. I hate Denmark.

PAUL: Bit harsh. Your Mother would be upset to hear you say that. Remember that Christmas supper we had; she cooked quail's eggs in duck fat.

Paul looks at him, takes a moment.

MARTIN: Not very slimming.

PAUL: It's your fault I became a sports fanatic.

MARTIN: You were already far gone. Or was it the lycra shorts that got you?

Paul has become nervous and starts pacing the room; his hands tremble and shake.

PAUL: It was my first proper Danish Christmas.

MARTIN: I remember it well.

PAUL: A great Christmas.

MARTIN: I hate the cold, always have done.

PAUL: You hated the winters and you were a miserable sod, even in England. Hey, remember that trip to Brighton we went on for half term?

MARTIN: It was over twenty years ago. I've thought of it often, especially that dirty hotel room we stayed in. You thought it was great.

PAUL: Romantic.

MARTIN: Scabies' aren't.

Paul is shaking very badly now, Paul goes over to him and holds his hands still. For a moment they stand looking at each other.

MARTIN: Are you all right?

PAUL: Actually, I'm not used to the cold.

MARTIN: You're hands are red hot.

PAUL: It's all the moving about.

Paul looks at him.

MARTIN: I don't think you cope here alone at all. It's ruining your health.

PAUL: That's not true, I'm fine. God keeps me company.

MARTIN: Maybe you need a change? I can recommend you for another job, some where else, where there are people.

PAUL: NO! No, don't do that, I'm all right.

MARTIN: I don't think so.

PAUL: Martin, don't. I need this job. I need to stay here.

MARTIN: I'm not making you unemployed; I'm offering you a chance to get out of here. Work somewhere else.

PAUL: No, I don't want to, I want to stay here.

MARTIN: I don't think you know what you want.

PAUL: Don't patronise me. I do a good job here, I like it here.

MARTIN: How can you like the isolation, the loneliness? You don't, you're kidding yourself. I think you've got to change your situation before it destroys you.

PAUL: Don't be so dramatic.

MARTIN: You're the one shaking.

There is an awkward pause. Paul tries to pull himself together. He picks up his bible.

MARTIN: New or old testament?

PAUL: So, how's your old man?

Martin eyes him up, realising he's got to bide his time.

MARTIN: You could say he's a changed man. During an operation 10 years ago he had an anorism on the operating table, they managed to save him but when he came round he was a completely different man.

PAUL: There was always room for improvement.

MARTIN: No, literally, he was changed, his personality. Like Jekyll & Hyde. He went in Soren Illemann but came out a monster.

PAUL: Wow!

MARTIN: My mother divorced him; he drank, was abusive, and spent all their savings. We have little to do with him now. He's re-married.

PAUL: So, how's your Mum?

MARTIN: She doesn't like me living in Greece. But then I'd rather live in a hot climate, and Athens suits me.

PAUL: And the Greek boys…

MARTIN: That's extra. What about you?

PAUL: Married, one son; Elliot seventeen. I married not long after we… we said…

MARTIN: Goodbye? (*Pause*) I suppose it's hard for us to avoid that subject…

PAUL: I'm divorced.

MARTIN: When did that happen?

PAUL: Just after Elliot was born. I moved out, and then applied for the Home Office job; I was moved to Denmark, of all places. I looked for you, but there was no internet back then. I couldn't find you.

MARTIN: You had my address.

PAUL: I spoke to your Mother, gave her my number to give you. Said she wasn't allowed to give out your number, not even to me. I hoped you would find me.

MARTIN: She gave it me. (*Pause*) I tore it up.

Paul looks at him and is visibly stung by this.

PAUL: Why?

MARTIN: You have to ask?

Martin gets up and gets some distance between them. They eye each other up.

MARTIN: How long were we together?

PAUL: (*He looks shocked, as if ready to bolt*) Two years.

MARTIN: Was it, as long as that?

PAUL: Last two years at University.

There is a long pause as the two men take swigs of their drinks.

PAUL: You have come here to get rid of me.

MARTIN: Nothing's been decided yet.

PAUL: Tell me the truth, you owe me that.

MARTIN: I owe you nothing.

Paul calmly sits down on his bed and rubs his head.

PAUL: You're not taking this place away from me, I need it.

MARTIN: For what? I could turn this station to automatic; there'd be no need for anyone to be here.

PAUL: I need to be here.

Paul, absent mindedly takes out the revolver from under his pillow and starts fiddling with it, Paul is very alarmed and slightly afraid.

MARTIN: Paul.

PAUL: You tore up my note, ripped it up, destroyed it, took it apart, smashed it, you fucking moron mouthed piss head, wanker.

MARTIN: It was more than twenty years ago, why are you so upset?

PAUL: I lived there for two years. It's not that big. You walk twice down Strandboulevarden and you know everyone.

MARTIN: I saw you, many times.

PAUL: You did? *(Paul has now put the gun in his hand and it looks as though he is ready to fire it. He waves it about in the air between them)* And you never came and spoke to me, what's that all about, have you any idea what you did to me?

MARTIN: You hurt me.

PAUL: So much so that you took to hiding up alleyways? I hurt me too, to the very core.

MARTIN: Is that why you've cloistered yourself up here? Hiding from the world, hiding from your feelings? Yeah, well you were always more capable of shoving your feelings down deep.

PAUL: Deep down. Deep down. Deep down. Get it right. You've always got to get everything right. The temperature outside, so you know how much to wear, the level of UV light so you wear the right goggles. The core depth, so you don't pollute the sample. Get it right. The temperature of the drill has to be right, so you don't melt the ice around your sample and contaminate it that way. Get it right! The climate in here, so the machines maintaining the temperature don't break down, so you don't wake up frozen to death.

MARTIN: You can't wake up if you're dead.

PAUL: How would you know if deep down you were already
dead? How would you know that your soul had already
turned to ice if you were already dead, dead deep down?

*They stand looking at each other Paul has now raised the gun
pointing it at Paul. They stand and stand.*

MARTIN: My English is better than your Danish.

PAUL: I wouldn't bet on that, I had lots of practice trying to find
you…

Det er jeg ikke så sikker på, jeg fik øvet mig meget mens jeg ledte
efter dig…

*Martin gets up and goes to the window, buying time; he was very
shocked at Paul's Danish. Paul still has the gun aimed at Martin,
even when he has his back to him.*

MARTIN: Where am I expected to sleep?

PAUL: Down the corridor in the other office but the heating
hasn't worked in there for months, I've told them to fix but
they haven't sent anyone to do it and I can't, as I don't have
the parts. Get it? Lack of support.

MARTIN: So where do I sleep?

PAUL: Well, after 20:00hrs the heating goes down really low all
over the building, the company's way of saving money and
the only room left with decent warmth is this one.

MARTIN: There's only one bed.

PAUL: There's a spare sleeping bag, you can use that.

The look of horror on Martin's face is almost comical.

MARTIN: I'll sleep in the other room.

He walks out. Paul is still standing there with the gun cocked, shaking.

PAUL: currens itaque Esau obviam fratri suo amplexatus est eum stringensque collum et osculans flevit

Then Esau ran to meet his brother, and embraced him: and clasping him fast about the neck, and kissing him, wept.

He looks at it still shaking.

BLACKOUT

Act 2
Scene 3

The wind whips against the walls of the station, in the dark, Paul tosses and turns. It's cold and gloomy, suddenly the door opens and Martin comes running in with his sleeping bag, dressed only in his long johns, he kicks his toe and searches around for somewhere to lay his bag. The only place is by the side of the bed, between the desk and the bed.

He settles down shivering and cursing in Danish. Finally he falls asleep as the wind gets louder outside. Paul looks down on him and gathers up his blankets and walks out of the room, hesitating at the door.

BLACKOUT

Act 2
Scene 4

Lights up. Paul is working at the laptop, the pile of CDs next to him. Martin is asleep on the floor in a sleeping bag. He stirs and sits up, rubbing himself.

PAUL: You'll get used to the weather.

MARTIN: I'm here for too short a time, in and out. I don't want to get used to it. My marrow froze two days ago.

PAUL: Your kidneys go next

MARTIN: What about my liver?

PAUL: Sometime tomorrow and we already know when your heart froze over.

MARTIN: (*He shoots Paul a look*) I'll be fine.

PAUL: Dream on, the cold and the whiteness do things to machines, people. The starkness and ice seep into your bones, your very soul. With machines they seem to be working, they are working, but then, something goes wrong, something was wrong right from the very start. You'll be lucky if you're out of here in a month. It's harsh here and only the adapted survive.

MARTIN: I won't need to adapt.

Jeg behøver ikke tilpasse mig.

PAUL: Oh, the old stubborn Martin is still in there.

Nå, den gamle stædige Martin er stadig derinde.

Martin looks at him, visibly shocked, not sure how to respond.

MARTIN: I can't sleep on this floor every night. I'll need to sort out the heating in the other room.

PAUL: That's what I mean, you'll get it to work, all right, but the moment you step outside the room, it'll break down. Or worse still after you've fallen asleep and you freeze to death. It's done it to me every time.

MARTIN: And you think that's because of the snow and ice.

PAUL: It gets in everything, the brazen white blandness of it all, it sucks at your soul out into it; you're devoured by it; eaten by it, chewed and spat out by it as slush, dirty, filthy brown slush.

Martin heads out the door.

MARTIN: I see.

He shudders as he looks at Paul.

PAUL: (*Shouting to be heard*) I've gone through some of the data and, there are a few mistakes.

MARTIN: (*Off stage*) We should both go through them and I'll make sure that you enter the new data correctly from now on.

Martin comes back in, getting dressed, and sits next to Paul and works. Paul is mesmerised by his hands.

MARTIN: When the correlation from the surface area is put in above the amount of liquid you should… what are you doing?

PAUL: Listening.

MARTIN: No, you weren't.

PAUL: I was.

MARTIN: You were looking at something.

PAUL: No, I wasn't, go on.

MARTIN: …of liquid you have at the boiling point.

PAUL: Then this gives you an approximation of the ice increase/decrease in the test area.

MARTIN: Yes. But if your measurement is off by even just 0.01% then it won't be correct. (*Paul looks at him*) What are you looking at?

PAUL: Nothing! I was just thinking.

MARTIN: About the mistakes you've made?

PAUL: I do double check.

MARTIN: You are looking at something.

Paul gets up and away from him, shaking, finally.

PAUL: (*Quietly, softly*) Your hands.

Martin holds them up and looks at them himself, as if for the first time.

MARTIN: What's wrong with them?

PAUL: Nothing.

MARTIN: Then can we concentrate and get this work finished. There are some readings from three weeks ago that don't make sense. *(Holding up the folder)* Is that a three or a five?

PAUL: Er, five.

MARTIN: Is this eight?

PAUL: Yes, it is.

Martin points at some numbers, Paul reads them out.

PAUL: Six, nine, three, point three, four, four, five.

MARTIN: Your handwriting is illegible; you should enter the details on the computer.

PAUL: You can't take a computer out on the ice.

MARTIN: The figures in this folder should match the ones on the computer though.

PAUL: You've got such beautiful hands.

MARTIN: Don't you think?

PAUL: Yes, *(Coming round)* About what?

MARTIN: The figures.

PAUL: They were the part of you… I liked the most. Sorry…

MARTIN: If we're going to get the re-calibration of the station correct then our input data has to be correct.

PAUL: Right, we have to get it right.

Martin looks startled.

MARTIN: Are you going to get the gun out again?

PAUL: (*Smiling*) What are you on about?

MARTIN: You waved a gun in my face yesterday.

PAUL: (*Smiling*) No, I didn't.

MARTIN: You damn well did. And don't do it again.

Paul gets up and goes to the bed, he takes out the gun. Martin jumps to his feet and tries to get away from him Paul walks towards him holding the gun aloft.

PAUL: What's the matter? Look it's not loaded.

MARTIN: Put it away, now!

PAUL: Or what? You'll fire me?

MARTIN: Paul do it, put it down.

PAUL: All right.

He puts the gun under the pillow and sits back down on the table again.

PAUL: I'm sorry if I pointed it at you.

MARTIN: Forget about it.

Martin sits down next to him. Paul can't stand it any more.

PAUL: Don't you want any breakfast; you just jump out of bed and start work?

MARTIN: I'll eat later.

PAUL: It'll get cold.

MARTIN: We're going to get this finished, so I'm not having a shower till later either.

PAUL: You can't, it's broken; I haven't had one for over a month. Not since the water heater packed in. I'd rather have it to drink and shave with. I mean who sees me here.

MARTIN: Don't worry we won't ever get that close.

There is a long pause.

PAUL: Want to hear something sick? Have you met my boss in London, Gordon Macdonald, fat, miserable, old fart; been in the civil service for years. Anyway he's only worked two days a week for years and years. They kept him on with full pay when they were looking for a new post for him.

MARTIN: For a fortune?

PAUL: £90,000 a year.

MARTIN: You're joking, how old is he?

PAUL: Fifty-five, wait it gets better. He went to his superiors the other day and said that all this work was getting too much for him.

MARTIN: Two days a week?

PAUL: They're all friends together so they say to him, 'what would you like to do Gordon?' He says 'work one day a week.'

MARTIN: They laugh at him…?

PAUL: What? No! They say 'fine, Gordon, you can work one day a week, how much would you like to earn?'

MARTIN: They ask him that?

PAUL: He says, 'I was thinking about £76,000 a year,' they say, 'yes, of course.'

Paul bursts out laughing; Martin sits there with his jaw wide open.

MARTIN: How English. That's not funny, it's disgusting. No wonder they riot in the summer in the cities there. So much inequality. They're putting the people to work in wheelchairs too.

PAUL: Pulling the buses, to save power.

MARTIN: Stupid and cruel.

PAUL: That's why it's so funny. You really would lose your mind if you took it seriously. The politicians don't. Every question time they try to out do themselves with 'jokes' and funny banter, who cares if it's peoples lives their using as ammunition and fodder.

MARTIN: I've got to go out and collect the core samples from yesterday.

PAUL: Take this *(Handing him the gun)* just to be safe.

MARTIN: *(Martin stares at the gun)* Thanks

He's out the door and Paul gets on with his work, when the video phone goes off. Paul answers it and we see a woman with her back to us, she is talking to someone who's with her, a plumber.

IDA: Utætheden begyndte i går, jeg ved ikke, et eller andet sted under vasken.

The leak started yesterday, I don't know, somewhere under the sink.

She turns to face the camera and we see a nicely turned out Danish woman, Paul's mother, Ida.

PAUL: Mrs Illemann! How lovely to see you.

IDA: Paul Cartwright, is that you? Oh my god it is you. How are you?

PAUL: I'm fine.

IDA: It's been years and years...hasn't it?

PAUL: More than twenty.

IDA: Yes, and how they flew by. What are you doing in Greenland? (*There is a dawning on her face, something shocking*) So, if you're there, then you've seen my Martin?

PAUL: (*Smiling*) Yes, we're working together.

IDA: (*Worried and distressed*) Oh, oh dear!

PAUL: (*Not registering her distress*) I used to man this station here, alone. We were a look out station for nuclear missiles being sent to Europe, now it's becoming a climate monitoring station. It's no longer a secret base so I can tell you all about it.

IDA: I see, how interesting...

PAUL: I've been here fifteen years and I'm used to my solitude now. So, having someone here has been a bit strange, especially my old friend Martin Illemann.

IDA: You're not involved with anyone? You're still a handsome man, Paul, you always were, no sense wasting what you've got, it won't last forever you know.

PAUL: Mrs Illemann you're making me blush.

IDA: You were always a joker. So you've seen Martin then? Funny he never mentioned you earlier when I spoke to him.

PAUL: He's out on the ice collecting samples.

IDA: (*Straight to the point*) You broke his heart, Paul, you broke it clean in two. I'm very worried he's seen you. It might upset him greatly.

PAUL: Mrs Illemann?

IDA: Don't interrupt. You made such a terrific couple. I was very sad when you broke it up. Of course I knew, he told me everything, back then, before, before... Oh, don't look like that; you should have come out. He spent that whole summer lying on his bed. He didn't eat, he hardly drank. I was very worried about him. He was wasting away, it all seems so long ago but it was really terrible. He wouldn't talk to anyone. It was awful to watch. And, really he's never been the same since. He was always my smiley happy go-lucky son. But since then there has been a cloud a black, thick cloud, that always threatened to break. To unleash something dreadful, something malignant.

PAUL: How do you know it was me?

IDA: A mother knows.

PAUL: He had other friends.

IDA: No, he didn't. There was no one else like you. He used to tell me everything but since that summer my relationship with him has not been the same.

PAUL: (*Small*) Sorry

IDA: When he got his exam results he applied for the job in the Government, got it and was gone. I've only seen him two or three times a year since then. He was supposed to be coming home to me when he was called to Greenland and, and to you… Sometimes I think he blames me for what happened between the two of you. At least that's what I think. I've almost lost my mind with the worry and ceaseless wonderings about what happened and what should've happened.

PAUL: I see.

IDA: He never spoke of you again. I'm worried this might upset him, seeing you.

PAUL: He's a grown man.

IDA: You never struck me as being so green, a coward, yes but not green. Being 'grown up' doesn't mean you don't have feelings. Don't you know that?

PAUL: What I mean is…

IDA: Be kind to him Paul; don't think that across the gulf of all these years he'll be over you, we can't be sure. We don't know, he might still harbour feelings and it would be disastrous if he became unbalanced again.

PAUL: I have no intention of…

IDA: I've enjoyed our little chat. Glad to see you doing so well, tell Martin to give me a call.

PAUL: Yes, of course, Mrs Illemann.

IDA: Oh, and for god's sakes, call me Ida.

She's gone leaving Paul spinning. He begins to shake violently. Martin comes in, carrying the gun.

MARTIN: I've put the core samples in the refrigerator; you might want to check them over. It is so cold out there; I don't know how you stand it…

PAUL: I've just spoken to Ida.

MARTIN: You did?

PAUL: She told me everything. I only finished it because you seemed so indifferent, cold, to me. I felt I was just a shag. I needed more from you.

MARTIN: (*Ignoring him*) I bored down an extra two metres today; it should give a clearer differentiation result. I don't think I contaminated any of them, I only did two core samples better to be safe than sorry.

PAUL: (*Shouting*) You hid and scuttled away from me.

MARTIN: What's got into you again? You didn't want me.

PAUL: You never wanted me.

MARTIN: I loved you.

PAUL: You never told me.

MARTIN: You never showed it.

PAUL: ICICLE.

MARTIN: Don't call me that.

PAUL: ICICLE! Just another freezing cold Dane. All jolly and happy, skipping through life, apparently carefree, more like couldn't careless.

MARTIN: (*Shouting, brandishing the gun*) And you're so warm and together?

PAUL: (*Shouting*) Icicle, stabbing in my heart. Look where I ended up? Here! Alone!

MARTIN: I thought your god kept you company.

PAUL: You broke my heart.

MARTIN: (*Shouting*) Your heart?

PAUL: (*Shouting*) You haven't got one.

MARTIN: (*Shouting*) You never had one.

PAUL: You never looked.

MARTIN: You never bothered.

PAUL: (*Yelling*) You never had one to lose!

MARTIN: (*Pointing the gun at Paul*) What do you know?

PAUL: You dumped me.

Martin roars and lunges for Paul, they fall over backwards, over the bed, and disappear in a tumbling mass of clothes and blankets. They appear wrapped in each others arms, struggling, cussing, sweating, and wrestling.

The gun goes clattering to the floor. They fall over again, the fight goes on, but this time when they come up, they grab each other and kiss each other roughly, angrily. They stop and look at each other, then kiss again, ripping at each others clothes. They begin to make love; a rough, violent love, where Martin takes Paul from behind and doesn't ease up. Like two dogs. The web cam flashes to life, it is Mr King. He looks about from the screen and fails to notice the two men, at it, at first.

KING: Ah, Dr Illemann, there you are, I just wanted to see if…
    stop that, stop fighting, it's disgraceful two grown men…
    fighting… (*He realises they're not fighting*)

We see that he realises what's going on, looks uncomfortable and signs off. We see Paul and Paul embrace in a long drawn out kiss, as the screen goes black and:

BLACKOUT

END OF ACT 2

INTERVAL

Act 3
Scene 1

Lights up on stage slow and low. Martin is in bed, he rolls over in just a pair of all in one leg warmers, and he's tussled, loved and very sexy. He sits up. We see Paul sitting on the floor behind the desk. Martin can't see him yet.

MARTIN: Paul?

There is no answer. Martin sits up and notices Paul on the floor. Paul throws the bible to the floor. Martin goes over to him and picks it up, kneeling down beside him.

MARTIN: Are you all right?

PAUL: I've sinned. He won't forgive me now.

Paul pushes his hand away and gets up to leave, Martin throws the bible back on the floor, grabbing hold of Paul, pulling him to him.

MARTIN: Calm down, I'm here.

PAUL: All these years I've hidden, hoping to quell these feelings. I've failed.

Martin motions them over to the bed and they sit down. Martin starts to kiss him and love him and, at first Paul, resists but then gives in and they collapse on the bed, in a fit of passion.

MARTIN: Thank god!

BLACKOUT

Act 3
Scene 2

We find Paul and Paul lying bed together, they are fast asleep an empty bottle of vodka next to them, one of them is snoring loudly.

The video screen flickers to life and flashes light into the room. It is Elizabeth. She looks around the room and sees the pile in the bed, in the gloom she's not sure what she's seeing. She thinks Paul is fast asleep.

ELIZABETH: Paul. Christ, wake up will you?

The screen goes blank.

Act 3
Scene 3

Singing is heard off stage, loud bawdy singing. Paul and Paul stagger in singing at the top of their voices a song in Danish. They are arm in arm both holding a bottle of gin and completely pissed-out of their minds.

PAUL:
MARTIN:

(Together)
Sejler op ad å'en
sejler nedad igen
Det var vel nok en dejlig sang
Den må vi ta' endnu en gang
(And again)
Sejler op ad å'en
sejler nedad igen
Det var vel nok en dejlig sang
Den må vi ta' endnu en gang

They stagger about, singing this song, and very often latch on to each other with their lips and snog. Until:

PAUL: Canterbury 1986.

MARTIN: January 1986, Neil Lovegrove.

PAUL: James McMahon. They were both South African.

MARTIN: Why'd they come with us?

PAUL: It was their car.

MARTIN: It snowed.

PAUL: A lot.

MARTIN: I remember, Yuk…

PAUL: I've still got the photos.

MARTIN: Did you have sex with Neil?

PAUL: No, I certainly did not.

MARTIN: I thought you did.

PAUL: You're the only man I've ever had sex with.

Martin hugs him close and kisses him.

PAUL: You're the free and easy one.

MARTIN: Don't confuse my Danish laissez afair with free and easy.

PAUL: You always flirted with James.

MARTIN: That's not the same as doing something.

PAUL: How do I know that?

MARTIN: Cause I'm telling you. Nothing happened. It was just flirting.

PAUL: Do you still behave like that? Flirty?

MARTIN: It was more than twenty years ago, I was a kid, all twenty-three year olds flirt.

PAUL: I didn't.

MARTIN: You've got your religion to thank for that. Why do you think we split up? Because of you! It was your fault. I couldn't deal with all the internalised homophobia. It was all that guilt, you could never relax, you're not relaxed now either.

PAUL: Such terrible guilt.

MARTIN: Let it go, Paul.

PAUL: I was terrified you'd dump me.

Paul pushes away from him.

MARTIN: I was in love with you, why would I have done that? I'd found my soul mate.

PAUL: You behaved like every other poofter, fucking everything in sight.

MARTIN: But I didn't.

PAUL: You never made it clear to me how you felt.

Martin marches up to him and grabs him, physically lifting him off his feet in a bear hug.

MARTIN: What's this? And this?

Paul pushes him away.

PAUL: Stop it.

MARTIN: It's affection, Paul. You wouldn't know it if it smacked you in the face. Your religion's taken that away from you, your ability to love and be loved as you choose and left you riddled with this guilt.

PAUL: You don't know what you're talking about. You only came to church with me once.

MARTIN: You only went once.

PAUL: I used to go with my Dad.

MARTIN: So, why are you complaining about me going to church?

PAUL: It was my first time since I was a kid. I wanted it to be something special.

MARTIN: It was; it was a lovely church, cathedral, abbey, chapel, basilica; synagogue, mosque, they're all the bloody same, a place to make you feel bad about yourself.

PAUL: You weren't supportive.

MARTIN: I don't like the dogma.

PAUL: Dogma!

MARTIN: Yes. The dogma…

PAUL: I've been searching, looking.

MARTIN: For what?

PAUL: I…I…hope.

MARTIN: Hope?

PAUL: Yes, for the future.

MARTIN: You were looking for god.

PAUL: Comfort, I wanted to be comforted.

MARTIN: There's no comfort.

PAUL: You shouldn't make fun…

MARTIN: It's hard not to. Beads, wigs, pork, fish, shell fish, covering up of women, Roman instruments of torture. It's about control.

PAUL: Structure.

MARTIN: For what?

PAUL: Civilisation.

MARTIN: Blowing yourself up? Eating sardines on a Friday? Killing innocent people?

PAUL: It's our choice… a life governed by faith.

MARTIN: Controlled by faith, by lies.

PAUL: So you say.

MARTIN: How many virgins do you know? And how many of them have given birth to children? All those years ago, when we were simple, ignorant, the myths were a good way of explaining the inexplicable. But now, now we have science. People have studied, taken evidence.

PAUL: Faith requires no evidence, no proof.

MARTIN: Yet you needed my proof. Proof that I loved you. Physical proof. My presence, my person to show I loved you. It wasn't enough that I still loved you, never stopped loving for all these years from a distance. That you required me to show up, prove to you how I felt. Quiet rightly too. So why accept, tolerate your god not showing up, being there when you want him.

PAUL: It's an act of faith. I can feel Him in my heart.

MARTIN: Then why've you never felt my love too?

There is a long pause, has Paul seen the light? Does he understand the point.

MARTIN: Like all religious people you're wrapped up in your self-righteous blanket and no one can get through.

PAUL: You're being rude.

MARTIN: Talking about a point of a religion is not rude.

PAUL: You're an atheist.

MARTIN: Yes, and how many atheists have you known to blow people up, burn them at the stake, poison them, draw and quarter them?

PAUL: It's not the point.

MARTIN: We're all human, Paul, all of us, descended from the same ancestors. All religion is part of a culture. If anything I can be accused of culturism, but I'm not even being that.

PAUL: You'll never understand. You don't know what it's like to be persecuted against.

MARTIN: I know just what it's like, I'm gay. There are lots of promotions that have mysteriously passed me by. I experience it at work all the time. In my everyday life I am marginalised. How many stories are out there about me? Every film, book, show, story has the hetero narrative rammed in there. Your people, have it all mapped out. The route planned, boring as it may be, but it forces you NOT to think, not to question.

PAUL: We all have an axe to grind.

MARTIN: Let's not argue, there's nothing to argue about.

PAUL: Your anti-religiousness gets in the way.

MARTIN: I love you.

PAUL: What?

MARTIN: Talk to me, explain it to me.

PAUL: You said you love me.

There is a pause.

MARTIN: Did I? Well, it was a slip of the tongue.

Paul moves away, shaking slightly.

PAUL: Like a friend, you mean?

MARTIN: I meant it? But, no, like a lover. It's not a sextræf.

PAUL: What?

MARTIN: Sextræf, it's a new word, sex date.

PAUL: But this is daft.

MARTIN: Well, now that you say that, perhaps it is daft! I loved
you all those years ago and in the last three weeks with what
we've had I've come to…to…

PAUL: (*Interrupting*) I don't know; it's not right is it?

MARTIN: There's nowt queer about love, Paul.

PAUL: It's easier for you, it always has been.

MARTIN: It's the most natural thing in the world. No one cares what you do in bed, no one.

PAUL: Not even you?

MARTIN: (*Smiling*) I'm a bottomist remember.

PAUL: Botanist. (*Trying not to smile*)

Paul moves closer to him and puts his arm around him, hugging, and kissing him.

The video screen flashes to life.

MARTIN: Will we ever have any privacy.

It is Mr King. He looks up at the two men, coughing and clearing his throat; Paul can't face it, he rolls his eyes and leaves the room.

KING: I just wanted see how the pair of you were getting along but I don't think I needed to worry.

MARTIN: Concerned about your station, then?

KING: You, actually.

MARTIN: Whatever? The supplies and parts are late again.

KING: Tell John.

MARTIN: The order was put in three weeks ago.

KING: Well, they should be there soon.

MARTIN: Good job! We've only got some tins of baked beans and some...

KING: Vodka!

MARTIN: Otherwise we'll starve to death.

KING: So, you and Paul are getting the samples up?

MARTIN: Amongst other things.

KING: I bet.

MARTIN: We were hard at it this morning.

KING: I'm sure.

MARTIN: You bet...

KING: Look, Illemann, what you do in private is your own business.

MARTIN: There's no privacy here, remember? This web cam is on 24/7. We can't turn it off this end.

KING: For your protection.

MARTIN: Then don't moan if you catch me wanking.

KING: We've got over the wanking but this business with Paul is all over London.

MARTIN: (*Trying to make light of it*) Like a rash?

KING: Like the pox and it's not good. You shit in your own backyard that's fine but not in my yard; sir, not mine. Do we understand each other?

MARTIN: Tell me something, if I were a woman, would we be having this conversation?

King reaches forward and flicks off the computer, his end.

MARTIN: Closet!

BLACKOUT

From the blackout we hear the distant rumble and whirr of a helicopter engine approaching the base. The noise gets louder and louder as:

Act 3
Scene 4

Lights flash up on stage, Martin and Paul are looking out the window, at the audience, watching the helicopter, getting nearer and nearer.

PAUL: About time.

MARTIN: If John's onboard, remind me to thump him.

PAUL: Oh, no that pleasure's going to be all mine, I owe him some slaps.

MARTIN: What's the bet they've forgotten the beef?

PAUL: I hope they've sent the pork.

MARTIN: For Jacob?

They smile at each other as the deafening roar of the helicopter stops and:

BLACKOUT

Act 3
Scene 5

Paul is talking to Elliot on the Videophone. He's more drugged fucked than before but Paul fails to notice.

ELLIOT: Mum hasn't told you about Mazz?

PAUL: No.

ELLIOT: It's this guy she's been seeing and he moved in with us about three weeks ago. He's Lebanese.

PAUL: Is he Muslim?

ELLIOT: No.

PAUL: Thank god.

ELLIOT: Dad! There's nothing wrong with being Muslim.

PAUL: Er, no of course not. But it would make an already difficult situation harder to deal with.

ELLIOT: Why? I've got lots of Muslim friends.

PAUL: You do? Good. Does he work?

ELLIOT: Says he's an architect but he sits around the house all day doing nothing. I'm always in my room; they're so lovey dovey; it's disgusting.

PAUL: I'll talk to your mother.

ELLIOT: I can't stand it, you're my Dad not him, I hate it when he tells me what to do, and they're drinking, a lot...

Paul tries to hide his vodka bottle.

PAUL: Are they? That's not good, I'll sort it out.

ELLIOT: Promise?

PAUL: Yes. Is your Mother around now?

ELLIOT: No, they've gone out in Mum's new car.

PAUL: What new car?

ELLIOT: An Audi.

PAUL: An expensive German car?

ELLIOT: (*Giggling*) I know, it's terrible.

PAUL: Where'd she get the money? Why am I asking?

ELLIOT: My new uniform for the last two years, my trousers are half way up my leg. And she's behind with my school fees.

PAUL: Why didn't you tell me this before? When I we spoke last?

ELLIOT: It's so rare I talk to you; that I didn't like bringing it up, I was afraid it would spoil our conversation.

PAUL: Do you know when they'll be back?

ELLIOT: No idea, last week they were gone the whole weekend, I had to fend for myself.

PAUL: Look, I'm really sorry about all this, I really am. I'll sort it out with your Mother.

Martin enters and for a moment Paul is a little uneasy, Elliot watches him cross the room.

PAUL: Elliot, this is Dr Martin Illemann, he's the new boss here. He runs a tight ship.

As Paul says this Martin comes over to the screen and plants a huge wet kiss on Paul's forehead, ruffling his hair, Paul looks at the computer screen and smiles, Elliot beams back.

MARTIN: Hi, Elliot, nice to meet you, I've heard a lot about you.

Martin continues leaning on Paul, who cannot do anything as he is frozen with shock.

ELLIOT: Are you two lovers?

There is a stony silence as Martin waits for Paul to respond, Paul continues to sit there solid and rooted to the spot.

ELLIOT: That's cool Dad, there's nothing wrong with it, just be careful...

Elliot smiles at them.

ELLIOT: Or get tested and then when you both know you're negative you can shag as much as you like.

Paul's jaw drops even lower.

MARTIN: So, how's school?

ELLIOT: Great, I've just finished a paper for Geography.

MARTIN: Do you like it?

ELLIOT: Yeah, I'm thinking of becoming a geologist.

MARTIN: Good for you, it's a great subject.

ELLIOT: But if I don't get the grades then I might move to London and join the army.

MARTIN: That's a change!

ELLIOT: I need to use my brains and my hands. I don't know; I've really no idea what I want to do yet.

MARTIN: Just get some qualifications under your belt and you can do anything.

ELLIOT: You're right there Dr Illemann.

MARTIN: For god's sake call me Martin.

ELLIOT: Ok, great, all right, I've gotta go. See you Dad, bye Martin, speak soon, have fun in the snow.

He gives them a great big wink. The screen goes blank.

MARTIN: Is he all right? He looks like he's on something…

PAUL: My god! My god! My god!

Paul gets up from the chair, circling the room, clutching the sides of his head.

PAUL: My god! My god! My god!

MARTIN: He can get help.

PAUL: My god! My god! My god!

MARTIN: Paul…

PAUL: I've just been outed to my family, discovered my seventeen year son's probably having sex and you talked more to him in those few minutes than I have in his entire life.

MARTIN: He seems like a sweet boy.

Paul collapses in great distress.

PAUL: What if he tells his mother? She'll cut off all contact for me with him. I don't want to lose my son.

MARTIN: She can't do that, he's an adult.

PAUL: I don't want to lose my son again...

Martin goes to him to comfort him but Paul shrugs him off, as Paul gets back on his feet again. He paces the room becoming more and more panicked.

MARTIN: Paul calm down, everything's all right.

PAUL: That's just it; nothing is, look at me I'm a wreck, terrified about what we're doing.

MARTIN: I think it's this place, it's got to you.

PAUL: I like it here, I always have.

MARTIN: You've adapted, but you're stunted.

PAUL: I like my own company.

MARTIN: It's not healthy.

PAUL: It doesn't bother me.

MARTIN: Because you've stopped noticing. Look at you, you're a nervous wreck.

PAUL: You make me nervous.

MARTIN: Rubbish… there's been talk for ages that you're not well. That was the reason for closing this down.

PAUL: So, you are getting rid of me?

MARTIN: More than likely.

PAUL: What about what we've been doing for the last month together.

MARTIN: We're having some fun.

PAUL: Fun! Is that it, some fun? I don't want some fun; I want to be, to be, loved. Don't you see? What am I saying? You'll shoot your load, do the job and then piss off back to Athens and your infant Greek lover, leaving me high and dry.

MARTIN: I don't know what's going to happen, neither do you.

PAUL: It's almost a god given certainty that you'll leave me, again.

MARTIN: (*Firm, angry*) Get it right, you left me.

PAUL: What difference does it make? I've always been alone and now, now that I've had it, it's going to be snatched away from me.

MARTIN: You could take it from me.

PAUL: Do you want it from me? Do you?

MARTIN: I… I don't know…

PAUL: (*Ignoring him*) I'm such a failure, a miserable lousy
father, a bunged up, stuffed up father, nothing comes out of
here right, nothing! (*Motioning his mouth*) I feel things, I
think things but they get short circuited before they get out of
my trap, they get caught in my throat. I feel like I'm on fire.
All I want to do is tell that boy I love him but I can't, I can't.
When he comes to me asking about love what am I going to
say, what? I don't know anything about it. I can't even tell
you what I want, what I need.

*Paul has worked himself into suck a pitch that he falls on the floor
tears streaming down his face. Martin goes over to him, but is not
sure what to do at first.*

*Martin gets on the floor with him and cuddles him; Paul falls into
his arms and sobs. For a while the two men remain there, Martin
trying his best to comfort and soothe his desperate friend.*

MARTIN: It's never too late, Paul, you can make it up to him,
you just have to want to do it.

*Paul looks up at him, wiping his tears and breathing more calmly,
he buries his head in Martin's arms and gets as much love as he
can before coming up for air.*

PAUL: I didn't have the heart to tell him we don't have condoms
here.

Paul looks down at him as the lights fade to black.

BLACKOUT

Act 3
Scene 6

From the blackout the whistling of the wind picks up and we hear the growling polar bear again, the bins are knocked over. And the growling gets louder, then fades away, the whistling wind gets louder. There's very little light on the stage. Paul is kneeling in front of his alter. He settles down to pray, reading from the bible, in Latin. Martin watches for a moment from the door as Paul reads.

PAUL: dilectus meus misit manum suam per foramen et venter meus intremuit ad tactum eius

My beloved put his hand through the key hole, and my bowels were moved at his touch.

surrexi ut aperirem dilecto meo manus meae stillaverunt murra digiti mei pleni murra probatissima

I arose up to open to my beloved: my hands dropped with myrrh, and my fingers were full of the choicest myrrh.

emarcuit cor meum tenebrae stupefecerunt me Babylon dilecta mea posita est mihi in miraculum

My heart failed, darkness amazed me: Babylon my beloved is become a wonder to me.

Paul turns a few pages and then:

PAUL: facies et uncinos ex auro

Thou shalt make also hooks of gold.

Martin holds back for a moment longer, then moves in and settles next to Paul.

He makes the motion to pray alongside him. Paul looks over at him and smiles; Paul puts his arm around him as Paul continues to pray. He stops, closes the book, removes his Talit Katan and Kipa, folding them neatly in front of him.

MARTIN: What are you doing?

PAUL: Hoping.

MARTIN: Praying?

PAUL: Hoping that it would do something for me.

MARTIN: Did it?

PAUL: No, it never did, never has.

Paul leans into Martin as we:

FADE TO BLACKOUT

Act 3
Scene 7

From the blackness we hear Elizabeth's voice, when the lights come up we see Paul looking pacing the room behind the laptop.

ELIZABETH: The money hasn't arrived again. I think you do it deliberately.

PAUL: It's admin, sometimes they're a bit slack, there's nothing I can do.

ELIZABETH: I've got bills to pay.

PAUL: You've got nothing left over from last month? (*Going to the screen*)

ELIZABETH: No, I don't.

PAUL: You've got through £5,000 in less than a month?

ELIZABETH: I'm raising Elliot!

PAUL: With my money, there's nothing stopping you going out and getting a job.

ELIZABETH: What would I do? I'm not qualified to do anything, and whose fault's that?

PAUL: You could have done whatever you wanted, no one stood in your way. I certainly didn't, you weren't interested in anything but shopping.

ELIZABETH: Don't start that again. Where are you? Come and look at the camera…

PAUL: Get rid of that guy.

ELIZABETH: Elliot told you…

PAUL: I'll gladly pay for Elliot but I'm not paying for you to live with some idiot.

ELIZABETH: He's not an idiot.

PAUL: Get him out Elizabeth; it's not fair on Elliot.

ELIZABETH: If Elliot has a problem with Mazz, then he should talk to me.

He crosses downstage to look at the screen, Elizabeth looks down at him.

PAUL: How can he do that? You're the adult; you can't expect him to talk to you about those sorts of things.

ELIZABETH: Mazzen's living here and that's that.

PAUL: Then he can pay his half the bills. What's wrong with you? I've paid for everything all these years, buying you that house, and still you do this to me, to us.

ELIZABETH: Unlike you Paul, I need sex, I need intimacy. You don't know what these things are, you never did. We only had sex twice in all the time we were together, so how can I expect you to understand how I feel.

PAUL: I do.

ELIZABETH: (*She laughs at him*) How? Have you smuggled an Eskimo woman into your camp? Or are you having an affair with that new boss of yours?

PAUL: What?

ELIZABETH: Look at you, you're pathetic, you always have been and you'll always will be...

PAUL: Elizabeth, I don't have to pay for you to look after Elliot. He's not a job. So, if you want to live with this guy then move into his house.

ELIZABETH: Elliot is seventeen; he's not expected to look after himself just yet.

PAUL: Then conduct your relationship with Matten...

ELIZABETH: Mazzen.

PAUL: Conduct your relationship with him in your own time, in his house.

ELIZABETH: He doesn't have one.

PAUL: Has he got a job?

ELIZABETH: He's looking for work.

PAUL: You should be setting an example.

ELIZABETH: What example did you set? You buggered off as soon as you could.

PAUL: I buggered off to keep a roof over your heads; it was the only thing that came up.

ELIZABETH: It was the first thing, bloody Greenland, who the hell wants to go there, it's a white wasteland. Nothing but snow and polar bears.

PAUL: How would you know, you've never visited.

ELIZABETH: Wild horses wouldn't drag me there.

PAUL: No, you made that clear in the beginning.

ELIZABETH: You could've had any job you wanted.

PAUL: It was the only job I could get. You wanted a divorce.

ELIZABETH: You still have to pay, the deal was until he's
    twenty-one, you work out much longer that is.

The screen goes blank, she's hung up. Paul slaps his head then slams the table in frustration.

BLACKOUT

Act 3
Scene 8

Lights up on Paul working on his notes, Martin comes in taking off his coat, he's happy and chatty, and Paul is not.

MARTIN: -45 out there again today, Christ I'll be glad to get out of here. God forsaken country, I've had enough. I'm sick and tired of being chilled to the core, to the bone. Don't know how you stand it. How's the notes coming?

PAUL: Fine.

MARTIN: What's up with you?

PAUL: I expect you'll work that out once you've left this god forsaken country.

Paul jumps to his feet and marches out. Martin rolls his eyes and pinches the bridge of his nose.

MARTIN: (*Shouting*) There's nothing attractive about a sulky middle aged man.

PAUL: (*Sticking his head around the door*) My feelings are my feelings, and you should respect them.

MARTIN: Very funny, you think you're so funny.

PAUL: Practice what you preach.

MARTIN: Oh and you do?

PAUL: I don't preach, I interpret.

MARTIN: Then interpretate this... (*Giving him the finger*)

Paul disappears again and Martin slumps in the chair, turning on the computer and tapping in a number, dialling his home. The screen flashes to life, and we see the inside of a room in Athens. The camera is at a funny angle and all we see is Socrates getting fucked from behind by another Greek boy, we only see their heads, but it is obvious what is going on. Suddenly, Socrates looks round and he tears away from the other guy, crossing the room in Athens and ripping the connection apart. The screen goes black and Paul slumps his head in his arms.

BLACKOUT

Act 3
Scene 9

The web cam flashes to life and we see Sharon, Elizabeth's mother staring into the camera.

SHARON: I hate these things, they're awful. Why can't I use a telephone? I don't want to look at him. *(She looks up and over the camera to someone who is obviously talking to her)* Well, why didn't you tell me he could hear me? It's not my fault, you should have said something before. *(She squints her eyes and looks down and at the camera)* Is he there now? *(The other person says something again)* I've no idea, all I can see is a room, an untidy room, a window and mountains of snow.

Paul walks into the room and goes to the screen.

PAUL: Sharon, this is a pleasant surprise.

SHARON: Who for? I hate these things. Get nearer the camera, I don't have my glasses.

He moves closer.

SHARON: I'll get straight to the point. These payments you make to Elizabeth have been getting later and later and it's not good enough. She's trying to run a household.

PAUL: I'm not talking to you about this, Sharon, it's none of your business.

SHARON: Elizabeth's my daughter so it is my business. I never understood why you had to go and live up there but that's no concern of mine.

PAUL: I'm glad you admit something isn't.

SHARON: Are you trying to be funny?

PAUL: Obviously not. Look, those payments are made through my work, there's nothing I can do. Elizabeth shouldn't spend the money she gets so recklessly. She should be more careful.

SHARON: She's done a great job on her own, I think.

PAUL: She's never been alone, I've always supported her financially.

SHARON: All we're asking is for the money to paid into her account on time.

PAUL: She should ask her new boyfriend for some money, they're living for free in the house I paid for.

SHARON: Now, you're being petty.

PAUL: I work here to support my child, not yours. She should be more responsible.

SHARON: She's a good mother.

PAUL: At spending my money.

SHARON: You've always been such a loser. I've never liked you, and never will, with your mean spirited ways. The only time I've seen you smile is when you were boarding the plane for Greenland.

PAUL: You should wonder why I was so happy…

SHARON: I couldn't careless.

PAUL: Just like your daughter.

SHARON: This conversation's going no where.

PAUL: Did you expect it to?

SHARON: No.

PAUL: I don't know why you bothered contacting me.

SHARON: I won't again, if I can help it. I've made my point. (*To the person in the room with her*) How do you turn this bloody thing off?

The screen snaps white.

BLACKOUT

Act 3
Scene 10

Martin is sitting on the bed. Paul comes in and puts down some papers on the desk. Not a word passes between them. Paul finishes what he has to do and then walks out again. Martin rubs his head in frustration.

The computer flashes to life and Ida is on the other end, smiling at Martin.

IDA: At last I catch you.

MARTIN: Hello Mum. Sorry about not getting back to you sooner but it's been a bit hectic here.

IDA: Yes, I know you're busy. How has it been with Paul?

MARTIN: I'll have to tell you when I am back in Athens.

IDA: Tell me now.

Paul enters and folds up his bible.

MARTIN: No, we shouldn't.

IDA: Why ever not? He can't understand.

PAUL: You'd be amazed how much I can understand and say, Ida.

He puts his bible in the box at the end of his bed. The first time it has been put out of view.

Paul exits, smiling.

IDA: I had no idea he spoke such good Danish.

MARTIN: Neither did I, at first.

IDA: Have you been helping him?

MARTIN: No, he could speak it when I arrived.

IDA: Impressive. Tell me, how have you been coping?

MARTIN: Coping?

IDA: Yes, being there with the cold, the snow. I know how you hate all that.

MARTIN: Fine, fine, no trouble at all really.

She looks at him, not sure whether to believe him or not.

IDA: You don't sound too sure.

MARTIN: I shall be glad to get back to civilisation, that's true.

IDA: We take it all for granted don't we?

MARTIN: What?

IDA: Being able to walk to the coffee shop, go for a stroll. See our friends. Have friends.

MARTIN: Yes, I suppose we do.

IDA: All of us.

MARTIN: I'd like to think I didn't.

There is a pause.

IDA: All right, we'll talk more when you're home. Bye son.

MARTIN: Bye Mum.

Martin moves away from the laptop and ponders for a moment, he then exits.

The video screen on the laptop flashes to life, it's Sharon, she is very upset. In her distress she seems to have forgotten how to use the web cam. She looks about the camera, tears streaming down her face.

SHARON: Paul! Paul! Paul!

PAUL: What is it?

SHARON: There's been a terrible accident, oh, god no, this is terrible.

PAUL: Calm down, tell me, what's happened? Is Elliot all right?

SHARON: Oh, god what am I going to do, it's so terrible, so terrible.

PAUL: SHARON!

SHARON: It's Elizabeth; there's been a car accident, a crash, a car crash...

PAUL: Where's Elliot?

SHARON: What are we going to do?

PAUL: Sharon? Answer me?

SHARON: How could God do this to us? Why has He done this to us?

PAUL: Elliot?

SHARON: He's here with me. *(She sobs)*

PAUL: Elizabeth?

SHARON: Dead! She's dead…

Sharon wails in agony and walks out of frame, leaving only the pattern of the wallpaper behind. Paul sits down, his eyes wide open. The wind whistles and wails to: as Elliot walks in to shot, crying. His face scratched and bloody.

Paul gets up and moves to jump at the screen.

PAUL:Son!

BLACKOUT

END OF ACT 3

Act 4
Scene 1

The web cam screen is showing static, white noise. It crackles and pops, a signal is trying to get through. Finally, a disembodied voice is heard, it is John.

JOHN: Dr Illemann? Dr Illemann? Can you hear me? Please Dr Illemann, answer this message. (*Finally the screen clears up and John is sitting there. He looks at the camera at his end*) We have a signal again. (*Behind him, Jesper tries to see over his shoulder into the room.*)

JESPER: Martin, Martin kom hen til kameraet.

Martin, Martin. Come to the camera.

(*To John*) Are you sure it's on and working?

JOHN: You can see the room can't you. Maybe he's on the ice.

JESPER: There's been no contact for nearly three weeks. It's not good.

JOHN: Yeah, well I told you not to let him stay up there on his own; it takes a particular sort of mind set to cope with isolation like that.

JESPER: We didn't think Mr Cartwright was going to be away so long.

JOHN: Have you spoken to Mr King about that? They've no idea where Paul is, they can't find him, nor his kid. They disappeared after the funeral and no ones heard hide nor tail of them since.

JESPER: King promised a replacement a week ago.

JOHN: No one will do it, not on their own.

Jesper looks into the camera at his end and his face looms large on the computer screen.

JESPER: I'm really worried about him, Martin comes over as strong and tough but he's not, he never has been…

The screen goes blank. The side door opens and Martin walks in, dressed for the ice. He removes his protective gear, the same gear that Paul wore, and flops down on the bed. He rolls about and stares at the ceiling. The wind howls outside.

He sits up and looks about, crosses the room and picks up the vodka bottle sitting on the table, there's only a drop left and he necks it. He then touches the computer and sits down looking at the blank screen. He leans forward and rests his head on his hands and in no time is fast asleep. The screen flickers to life and flashes light across the top of his sleeping head.

The image dances about before solidifying, it is Ida Illemann. She looks at him and speaks but no sound comes out, we only have picture. She taps the camera and computer her end and speaks some more, still we don't hear what she is saying. She becomes increasingly agitated as she does not know that the sound is off at this end, in the station. She begins to think that Martin is ill or, or something worse. Her panic is extremely evident when, suddenly, the screen goes blank again, leaving Martin alone in the room.

He stirs and looks up, his sleepy eyes betraying his fatigue. He gets up and goes to the bed; rummaging around underneath he pulls out a fresh bottle of vodka and rips into it. He flops down on the bed and drinks some more.

He cradles the bottle and then rolls over, with his back to the screen, just as the computer flashes to life. Again it is Ida; she is relieved to see that Martin has moved. She speaks but still there is no sound. She fiddles with her computer and the sound begins to crackle and pop through.

IDA: Martin, Martin, answer me, what's the matter with you? I've been worried sick, I called just now, is there something wrong with the sound? Martin, wake up, answer me. Oh, darling, I am so worried about you. Please don't do this. It's not worth it.

She stares into the room, at her son lying on the bed and waits for an answer. She waits and waits.

IDA: I'm here if you need me, call me back. I love you.

She hangs up. Martin rolls over and staggers up across the room and turns the lap top computer away from the room, to face the audience, directly, he wants nothing to do with it. He walks out of the room, just as the screen flashes to life, it is Socrates.

He walks towards the web cam in his room; he is dressed in a coat, a bag over his shoulder, with his sunglasses on. He is very angry.

SOCRATES: You can have your stupid flat back and everything you've ever given me. I'm out of here and don't contact me ever again.

The screen goes blank.

Martin appears in the doorway, he did hear what Socrates said. He takes a long hard slop from the vodka.

MARTIN: Rend mig I røven!

Fuck you too!

He disappears out of the room.

The screen flashes to life it is Mr King.

KING: Dr Illemann? This is Mr King, I would be very grateful if
you would return my calls as soon as possible. Your lack of
communication is causing a lot of concern here in London.
We're preparing a flight to you within the next week but the
inclement weather is still too severe to risk a helicopter trip.
So, please contact us and let help in any way we can.

*He pauses, looking awkward for a moment and then the screen
goes blank.*

*Instantly the screen crackles and pops back to life. It is Sharon,
she is shouting and at first we can't hear what she is saying.*

SHARON: (*To the person she is with*) Shut up, I'll speak when I
want to. Paul! Paul! Answer me! Come to this damn machine.
You can't do this to me, you have no right. I think it's
disgusting. This is the only way of speaking to the
department that Paul Cartwright works for. I've got no other
number. I'm wracked with worry I don't know where my
grandson is. I've heard nothing from them and I suspect Paul
has something to do with this. I have rights and I demand
someone there does something about it. Hello! Hello! (*To the
person in the room with her*) All I can see is a window
looking out on all that disgusting snow, there's not even a
single bush there…

The screen goes blank, crackling and popping.

*Flashing on the screen is Jesper. He sits down in front of his
camera, looking out at the view of the snow.*

JESPER: Please, Martin, get in touch with base, you must explain what's happened to you; you might lose your job otherwise. Even the guys in the Danish Government are starting to lose their patience. They still can't get through to you because of the weather.

The screen goes blank.

All that is left in that empty room is the furniture and the howling wind outside. For moment after moment, we get a feeling of the sheer and utter isolation of the station, the bleakness, the wretchedness of the place, when, suddenly the screen, flashes to life and it is Paul.

He is looking around at what he is doing his end, he looks up at the camera and straight out to the audience. He pushes a few buttons and we hear the sound at his end. He clears his throat. We see that he is uncomfortable about something. He feels guilty about something.

PAUL: Martin? Hej Martin, it's Paul. Where are you buddy? Hej Martin, det er Paul. Hvor er du, kammerat? I suppose I should say sorry first of all for not contacting you sooner. But after the funeral there were lots of things I had to do and I wanted to spend time with Elliot and get my head sorted out. It was a horrible shock for them. She was in the car with Mazz, he was killed too, and they came off the road and smashed into an on coming car; killing the family in the other car outright. Mazz and Elizabeth were drunk, really drunk. There's a horrible investigation with the police we're going through. I was allowed to leave England for a while and I've brought Elliot here, to Spain. I thought he deserved it. *(Long pause)* I haven't gone back to work yet and I haven't contacted them. Don't tell them you've heard from me, please. When I get back to London I'll call you, not sure when that'll be. Take care.

He looks up at the screen, tempted to say something else but he doesn't. The screen goes blank as Martin comes tearing back into the room, eyes wide with panic and fear, he dashes to the computer, spinning it around. He hammers away at the thing, he looks at the screen, nothing. Martin is very distressed he sighs, holding back the tears.

MARTIN: No, No! Paul!

He slumps forward drunk and very distressed. The screen flashes to life and we hear the voice of Jesper.

JESPER: Nå, der er du. Vi har været enormt bekymrede, hvorfor har du ikke....

There you are we've been worried sick, why haven't you...

MARTIN: Lad mig være I fred.

Leave me alone.

He severs the connection. He gets up to leave but thinks better of it, what if Paul calls him back. He goes to the computer and turns it around and settles down, determined to answer it should another person call, just in case it is Paul. He doesn't have long, as King's face appears on the screen.

KING: Dr Illemann, there you are. We've been very concerned as to your welfare.

MARTIN: You mean the welfare of this place. I'm not an idiot.

KING: We're sending a helicopter to you later this week. As you know the weather there has been very bad. *(Pause)* I need to ask if you've heard from Paul Cartwright.

MARTIN: Paul Cartwright? Paul Cartwright? How many Paul's are there here, King? Three? Four? Where are they? Let me just have a look. No, there aren't any under the bed, there aren't any in the toilet and I didn't see one in the kitchen this morning. I didn't pass one in the refrigerator yesterday either. Maybe there's one hiding in the closet. Paul! Oh Paul! Come out, come out wherever you are.

KING: (*To someone he is with*) I think it's worse than we thought; he's out of his fucking mind.

Martin dashes back to the computer, instinctively; King backs away his end, eyes bulging.

MARTIN: There's nothing wrong with my mind, it's my life that's fucked up, you fool.

KING: Have you heard from Paul?

MARTIN: What if I have?

KING: (*To the person he's with*) I can't get a straight answer out of him.

MARTIN: (*Sarcastic*) That's because I'm not straight, Mr King, remember?

KING: Just hold out there Doctor, we'll have someone with you as soon as we can.

MARTIN: You do that...

Martin turns off the connection. The screen goes blank.

BLACKOUT

Act 4
Scene 2

In the blackout we hear the growls and rummaging about of the polar bear, it sounds so close and frightening. In the blackout we hear Martin fumbling about, we hear the gun cock. A flashlight is turned on; Martin gets up from his bed, flashlight in one hand the gun in the other. The noises seem to be just outside the door. Martin moves closer to it and listens. He's still slightly drunk; the sounds go on and then die down. He visibly relaxes for moment when there is a god almighty crash.

MARTIN: Jacob! Leave me alone. There's no more food.

He snaps the door open, roaring, shouting himself, letting off a few rounds from the gun. A loud polar bear roar is heard and Martin staggers back into the room, slamming the door behind him.

MARTIN: Go away! He's not here any more.

He collapses in a heap on the bed. Breathing heavily, terrified out of his life.

MARTIN: He's gone, left us. He's not coming back.

BLACKOUT

Act 4
Scene 3

Martin is looking at the computer. He finds the last transmission from Paul and plays it back, watching it mesmerised. We see that he is uncomfortable about something. He feels guilty about something.

PAUL: Martin? Hej Martin, it's Paul. Where are you buddy? Martin? Hej Martin, det er Paul. Hvor er du, kammerat? I suppose I should say sorry first of all for not contacting you sooner. But after the funeral there were loads of things I had to do and I wanted to spend time with the kids and get my head sorted out. It was a horrible shock for them. She was in the car...

Paul stops the machine and replays a part of it.

PAUL: Martin? Hej Martin, it's Paul. Where are you buddy Martin? Hej Martin, det er Paul. Hvor er du, kammerat? I suppose I should say sorry first of all for not contacting you sooner...

Martin rewinds it and plays part of it as a loop.

PAUL: Martin? Hej Martin, it's Paul. Where are you buddy?

PAUL: Where are you buddy? Hvor er du, kammerat?

PAUL: Where are you buddy? Hvor er du, kammerat?

PAUL: Where are you buddy? Hvor er du, kammerat?

PAUL: ...buddy? Kammerat

PAUL: ...buddy? Kammerat

PAUL: ...buddy? Kammerat

PAUL: ...buddy? Kammerat

Paul stops the loop and zooms into Paul's face.

MARTIN: Bastard.

BLACKOUT

Act 4
Scene 4

Martin has slumped in front of the computer screen. It flickers to life and it is Paul, who looks down at him for a moment. He smiles at his friend, fast asleep. When he does speak it is soft and quiet.

PAUL: Martin. Wake up Martin.

Martin stirs and looks up.

MARTIN: Paul.

PAUL: How are you? You look terrible.

MARTIN: Fine. Fine.

PAUL: Liar. Did you get my message?

MARTIN: Yeah, yes, thanks.

Martin is still asleep and then comes to his senses.

PAUL: Has the weather cleared up there?

MARTIN: Don't call me and act like nothing's happened. You should never have left without making up first. It's one of our rules.

PAUL: 'Our rules?'

MARTIN: I've been worried sick, incapacitated with worry.

PAUL: And vodka by the looks of it.

MARTIN: Don't try to be funny with me, it's not funny.

PAUL: Ok! Ok! I'm sorry, I really am.

There is a long pause.

MARTIN: Are you coming back?

PAUL: I don't know. I've got Elliot to think about. I go back to London tomorrow and face the music. I'm not sure how they're going to respond.

MARTIN: You're a security risk. They won't let you go just like that.

PAUL: What are you saying? I've got to watch my back?

MARTIN: You have to be careful.

PAUL: Well, I'll find out tomorrow.

There is another long pause as Paul looks at him and then away.

MARTIN: What about us?

PAUL: I don't know. It didn't work twenty years ago, why should it work now?

Another pause, as the enormity of what Paul has just said sinks into Martin's head.

MARTIN: That's it?

PAUL: What do you think?

MARTIN: (*Small, painful*) I love you.

PAUL: (*Gentle*) But is that enough?

They look at each other for a while, not saying another word. Martin reaches over, touching the screen, trying to reach his friend but then severs the connection. Martin slumps into his hands and sobs.

BLACKOUT

Act 4
Scene 5

Lights up to find Martin lying on the bed, he's now only dressed in his long johns. He's clutching a half empty bottle of vodka. The wind has died down, so only he makes any noise. His head falls back on the bed as he takes one last drink from the bottle. He passes out.

BLACKOUT

Act 4
Scene 6

The computer screen flashes to life and various images flash across it, Ida, Paul, King, Socrates, Jesper, John, Elliot, Elizabeth, Sharon, and even the outside world. It's as if the computer is dreaming, trying to make sense of everything that has happened. There are images of Elliot laughing, Elliot yelling, Elizabeth crying, King looking disgusted, and Socrates flipping us off. The sound is mixed up and jangled, nothing makes sense. It's bedlam, and over the top of this we hear, on the computer, the sound of a helicopter coming into land. A final image appears on the screen, it is Paul, just as the lights come up and the real Paul walks into the room. The real helicopter has just landed.

He stands just in the doorway, looking down on Martin. He then crosses the room and looks through some paper work. The rustling of the paper stirs Martin from his drunken slumber. He sits up and round, squinting, still blind drunk. He looks over at Paul.

MARTIN: Those new set of results are not conclusive. I think I contaminated the core sample when I was bringing it up.

PAUL: I am sure your whole system is contaminated, with booze.

MARTIN: Perhaps…

PAUL: The numbers look all right to me.

MARTIN: Wait! (*Rubbing his eyes*) Wait, you're here, not on the screen. You're not on the web cam, not just an image.

PAUL: I'm here, Martin.

MARTIN: Oh, god.

Martin staggers to his feet and lunges over the room towards Paul, we're not sure if he's up for a fight or what, at first. Paul stands his ground and catches Martin in his arms.

MARTIN: You came back.

PAUL: Yes, of course I did, you old fool. Do you think I'd leave you here in this godforsaken place?

MARTIN: You came back.

Martin is desperately trying to sober up, he pulls away from Paul.

MARTIN: But you didn't come back for me, you came to sort your things out, you're leaving.

PAUL: We'll talk about this later, you're too drunk.

MARTIN: Bastard. You're doing it again, you're dumping me.

PAUL: (*Going to him*) Lie down, sleep.

MARTIN: Get away from me, I can't stand it.

He staggers and falls across the room, and heads out the door. As the web cam flashes to life, it is King.

KING: Paul?

PAUL: Yes, I'm here.

KING: How is it?

PAUL: I've only just arrived, it'll take me a couple of days to sort through everything, and I'll get back to you.

KING: The place still looks like a bomb hit it.

PAUL: (*Under his breath*) I think one did.

KING: What was that?

PAUL: I'll get back to you. I need some time.

KING: You've got five days before your replacement arrives.

PAUL: Replacements, you mean.

KING: The sooner you're out of there the better.

The screen flashes off.

PAUL: I couldn't agree more.

BLACKOUT

Act 4
Scene 7

Paul is working away at the desk and laptop when Martin enters.
He is getting ready to go out on the ice. He picks up the radio,
walkie talkie; then rummages around in the drawer for the gun.

PAUL: We've run out of ammo. We didn't order any new rounds.
And I didn't bring any with me.

MARTIN: I haven't seen that damn bear around for weeks.

PAUL: He should have gone further north, now the waters finally
frozen over.

MARTIN: Do you think so?

PAUL: You should be all right, take it with you, if you're nervous.
Wave it about and scream a lot; that works just as well.

MARTIN: Maybe we should go out together.

PAUL: I have this report and collation to finish. I've only got
three days left here and it's taking ages to finish everything
up. You did nothing for weeks.

MARTIN: Well, I did, drink!

PAUL: For Denmark from the looks of it.

MARTIN: You must be glad to be leaving.

PAUL: I have no choice, my son needs me; I can't leave him
again. I did that once I won't and can't do that now. I have to
look after him. Be there for him.

MARTIN: I'll go and do that core sample.

Martin moves towards the door, putting his gloves on. Paul turns to look at him, to say something, but thinks better of it and watches him leave. He then goes back to his work. The outer door slams shut and Paul looks up; then carries on working. He sits there for a while.

Suddenly, there is a roar and a bang from outside, Paul turns round getting to his feet; he doesn't wait to hear any more, he dashes for the box, pulling out the huge hunting knife and then he's out the door.

When he has gone we hear shouts and yells and a blood curdling roar.

Martin comes staggering back in, his clothes ripped and torn to shreds. He sits panting on the bed, terrorised beyond belief.

We wait and wait and then Paul comes back in carrying the knife, covered in blood, dripping red everywhere. Martin stands staring for a moment. He looks down at the knife and then down at Paul. Paul drops the knife and runs to Martin.

Paul works quickly to get the jacket off, terrified there is terrible damage. Martin is coughing and choking from shock. Paul rips his clothes off and turns him round checking him over for cuts and bruises. He takes everything off, carefully inspecting and looking. At first he fails to notice Martin looking at him. Then he sees him and looks straight at him. There is no physical damage.

PAUL: (*His throat high and dry*) Thank God, no damage.

MARTIN: Is that all you're looking for?

PAUL: I don't think so.

MARTIN: Neither do I. What about Jacob?

PAUL: He's dead, I killed him.

Pause.

MARTIN: You saved my life…

Paul reaches to him and kisses him. Paul kisses him back and they fall back onto the bed locked together.

BLACKOUT

Act 4
Scene 8

The two men are lying on the single bed together. They are staring at the ceiling. Paul gets to his feet.

PAUL: This bed is too small for both of us.

MARTIN: (*Smiling*) For sleeping on, yes.

PAUL: (*Smiling back*) We've got all these damn reports to finish.

MARTIN: They can wait, if we're late, who cares?

PAUL: I'd like my last work here to be good. I need to finish off ready in time for my replacements.

MARTIN: I'll help you. (*Getting to his feet*)

They settle down to work at the desk.

MARTIN: Do you know who the replacements are?

PAUL: A man and a woman. They're not taking any more chances this time, and they're both married to someone else.

MARTIN: What difference will that make?

PAUL: You're right.

MARTIN: I thought the British Military were out of the closet now.

PAUL: Officially they are, but unofficially they're still in there, hiding amongst the coats.

MARTIN: And stockings.

PAUL: That's another department.

MARTIN: What about us?

There is a long pause as we wait for the answer to the question; both men busy themselves with their tasks until:

PAUL: Where are you going to go? Back to Athens?

MARTIN: No.

PAUL: You've got no idea where you're going do you?

MARTIN: I know where I'd like to go.

PAUL: Let me guess.

MARTIN: You never will.

PAUL: They speak English there?

MARTIN: Yes.

PAUL: There are pubs there?

MARTIN: Yes.

PAUL: Bacon for breakfast?

MARTIN: Yes.

PAUL: And a teenager?

MARTIN: What if he doesn't like me?

PAUL: We'll cross that bridge when we come to it.

In the distance a helicopter swoops closer and closer. Paul takes hold of Paul's hand.

PAUL: Dine hænder er kolde.

Your hand's cold.

MARTIN: varmt hjerte.

…warm heart.

The helicopter gets nearer and louder. Paul motions to leave and Martin nods, they walk out together hand in hand.

END

www.ingramcontent.com/pod-product-compliance
Lightning Source LLC
Chambersburg PA
CBHW072143280526
45788CB00002B/766